How IT Managers Can Get The Most Out Of Their Careers

Tips And Techniques That IT Managers Can Use In Order To Have A Successful Career

"Practical, proven techniques that will help you to manage your IT Manager career successfully"

Dr. Jim Anderson

Published by:
Blue Elephant Consulting
Tampa, Florida

Printed in the United States of America

Library of Congress Control Number: 2017901667

ISBN-13: 978-1542897013

ISBN-10: 1542897017

Warning – Disclaimer

The purpose of this book is to educate and entertain. This book does not promise or guarantee that anyone following the ideas, tips, suggestions, techniques or strategies will be successful. The author, publisher and distributor(s) shall have neither liability nor responsibility to anyone with respect to any loss or damage caused, or alleged to be caused, directly or indirectly by the information contained in this book.

<u>Other Books By
The Author</u>

<u>Product Management</u>

- Managing Your Product Manager Career: How Product Managers Can Find And Succeed In The Right Job

- How Product Managers Can Sell More Of Their Product: Tips & Techniques For Product Managers To Better Understand How To Sell Their Product

<u>Public Speaking</u>

- Creating Speeches That Work: How To Create A Speech That Will Make Your Message Be Remembered Forever!

- How To Organize A Speech In Order To Make Your Point: How to put together a speech that will capture and hold your audience's attention

<u>CIO Skills</u>

- How CIOs Can Bring Business And IT Together: How CIOs Can Use Their Technical Skills To Help Their Company Solve Real-World Business Problems

- New IT Technology Issues Facing CIOs: How CIOs Can Stay On Top Of The Changes In The Technology That

Powers The Company

IT Manager Skills

- How IT Managers Can Use New Technology To Meet Today's IT Challenges: Technologies That IT Managers Can Use In Order to Make Their Teams More Productive

- How To Build High Performance IT Teams: Tips And Techniques That IT Managers Can Use In Order To Develop Productive Teams

Negotiating

- Getting What You Want In A Negotiation By Learning How To Signal: How To Develop The Skill Of Effective Signaling In A Negotiation In Order To Get The Best Possible Outcome

- Exploring How To Get The Deal That You Want In A Negotiation: How To Develop The Skill Of Exploring What Is Possible In A Negotiation In Order To Reach The Best Possible Deal

Miscellaneous

- How To Heal A Broken Leg – Fast!: Understanding how to deal with a broken leg in order to start walking again quickly

- How Software Defined Networking (SDN) Is Going To Change Your World Forever: The Revolution In Network Design And How It Affects

Note: See a complete list of books by Dr. Jim Anderson at the back of this book.

Acknowledgements

Any book like this one is the result of years of real-world work experience. In my over 25 years of working for 7 different firms, I have met countless fantastic people and I've been mentored by some truly exceptional ones. Although I've probably forgotten some of the people who made me the person that I am today, here is my attempt to finally give them the recognition that they so truly deserve:

- Thomas P. Anderson
- Art Puett
- Bobbi Marshall
- Bob Boggs

Dr. Jim Anderson

This book is dedicated to my wife Lori. None of this would have been possible without her love and support.

Thanks for the best 21 years of my life (so far)...!

Table Of Contents

It's Your Career: Get The Most Out Of It

As an IT manager one of your most valuable possessions is your career. At your firm, you are the only person who is going to be spending any time worrying about your career: how's it going, what is your next step, what could you be doing better? These are all vital questions for you to be able to answer if you want to advance in your career.

We do need to be careful as we manage our careers. Not everyone that we work with may have our best interests in mind. Sabotage is always possible if we are not keeping our eyes open. Stay aware at all times and perhaps even take a look at how top athletes manage their careers in order to better understand what you should be doing.

The job that you have today may not be the job that you'll have tomorrow. That means that at some point in time you'll have to go looking for your next job. Do you know how to go about doing this without screwing up your current job?

None of us is perfect, we all make mistakes. As an IT manager you need to have a plan in place for dealing with the mistakes that you know that you'll eventually make. To make yourself more valuable to the company, you may want to consider getting an executive MBA. Picking a school and a program can be a real challenge.

One of the things that IT managers do a lot of is make presentations. The challenge that we face in doing this is that few of us have ever been trained how to do it effectively. We need to find out how to create better PowerPoint slides. A little bit of help in how to go about selecting the right colors to use wouldn't hurt either.

If you find yourself in a situation where your job has gone away either due to a restructuring, a layoff, or perhaps a merger, your #1 job is going to be to find your next job. Outplacement services might be made available to you and if so, you're going to have to know how to maximize this valuable resource.

For more information on what it takes to be a great IT manager, check out my blog, The Accidental IT Leader, at:

http//www.TheAccidentalITLeader.com

Good luck!

- Dr. Jim Anderson

About The Author

I must confess that I never set out to be a CIO. When I went to school, I studied Computer Science and thought that I'd get a nice job programming and that would be that. Well, at least part of that plan worked out!

My first job was working for Boeing on their F/A-18 fighter jet program. I spent my days programming fighter jet software in assembly language and I loved it. The U.S. government decided to save some money and went looking for other countries to sell this plane to. This put me into an unfamiliar role: I started to meet with foreign military officials and I ended up having to manage groups of engineers who were working on international projects.

Time moved on and so did I. I found myself working for Siemens, the big German telecommunications company. They were making phone switches and selling them to the seven U.S. phone companies. The problem was that the switches were too complicated. Customers couldn't tell the difference between one complicated phone switch from another complicated phone switch. Once again I found myself working with the sales and marketing teams to find ways to make the great technology that the engineers had developed understandable to both internal and external customers.

I've spent over 25 years working as an senior IT professional for both big companies and startups. This has given me an opportunity to learn what it takes to manage and IT department in ways that allow it to maximize its output while becoming a valuable part of the overall company.

I now live in Tampa Florida where I spend my time managing my consulting business, Blue Elephant Consulting, teaching college courses at the University of South Florida, and traveling to work with companies like yours to share the knowledge that I have about how to create and manage successful IT departments.

I'm always available to answer questions and I can be reached at:

Dr. Jim Anderson
Blue Elephant Consulting
Email: jim@BlueElephantConsulting.com
Facebook: http://goo.gl/1TVoK
Web: http://www.BlueElephantConsulting.com/

"Unforgettable communication skills that will set your ideas free…"

Create IT Departments That Are Productive And A Valuable Asset To The Rest Of The Company!

Dr. Jim Anderson is available to provide training and coaching on the topics that are the most important to people who have to manage IT departments: how can I build a productive IT department (and keep it together) while at the same time providing the rest of the company with the IT services that they need?

 Dr. Anderson believes that in order to both learn and remember what he says, speakers need to laugh. Each one of his speeches is full of fun and humor so that what he says "sticks" with everyone.

Dr. Anderson's CIO Skills Training Includes:

1. How to identify and attract the right type of IT workers to your IT department.
2. How to build relationships with the company's senior management in order to get the support that you need?
3. How to stay on top of changing technology and security issues so that you never get surprised?

Dr. Jim Anderson works with over 100 customers per year. To invite Dr. Anderson to work with you, contact him at:

Phone: 813-418-6970 or
Email: jim@BlueElephantConsulting.com

Blue Elephant Consulting

Speaking   Negotiating   Managing   Marketi

Chapter 1

How Can An IT Manager Get Ahead At Your Company?

Chapter 1: How Can An IT Manager Get Ahead At Your Company?

If we agree to take a step back from the world of IT for just a moment, how about if we spend just a bit of time talking about your career. How's it going? Are you where you'd like to be right now? Perhaps more importantly, have you been seeing your peers do better than you lately? Us IT Managers are generally pretty good at the technical side of doing our jobs; however, when it comes to managing our careers we are all too often just a bit clueless. Good news, some smart folks have been thinking about this problem and they have some suggestions to help us...

Geoff Colvin has written a great book called Talent Is Overrated in which he talks about just what it takes to be successful. He's got some good news for us and some bad news. Which would you like first? Let's start with the good news. All too often we tend to think that genetics plays a large role in somebody's success. In sports we have Tiger Woods, Michael Jordan, Lance Armstrong and in business we have Jack Welsh, Richard Branson, and even Warren Buffet. Clearly all of these folks must have come from amazing genetic stock, right?

Colvin throws this idea out the door. Yes, sports superstars probably do have some natural talents that help them during their career; however, that's not what made them a superstar. In business, if you've ever seen pictures of the really BIG names, then you'd quickly understand that they don't LOOK like they are anything special. However, Colvin says that great performance (from which comes great success) basically rests on one specific action more than anything else: deliberate practice.

Let's be real clear what is meant by practice here. We're not talking about going out and hitting 2,000 golf balls on a practice tee and then declaring that you are as good as Tiger Woods.

We're not talking about hosting and running 1,000 business meetings and then telling the world that you have Sir Richard Branson's leadership skills. Nope, what we are really talking about is practicing with a focus. This means that you hit a ball / run a meeting and at the end you sit back and ask yourself "...what could I have done better?" You then make a change in how you hit a ball / run a meeting and then you do it again. You ask the same question at the end of the activity and repeat it over and over again. Just in case you are missing this subtle point: this is no fun to do whatsoever. However it is necessary if you want to be better.

Colvin pointed out two great examples of people who have done just exactly this and gone on to greatness. The first is Jerry Rice who was an NFL wide receiver who wasn't really all that big nor was he really all that fast (in comparison to the other wide receivers on the field with him). However, Jerry noticed that by the end of a football game, all of the players on the other team were totally exhausted. Jerry spent the time focused on one thing: building up his endurance. What this meant is that when everyone else had nothing left to give, he had an extraordinary advantage over them during the final 15 minutes in the game. He used this advantage to score, score, score. Colvin also talks about the comedian Chris Rock. Chris is a huge star and puts on shows in large stadiums. However, long before those shows, he spends months going from small comedy club to smaller comedy club in order to practice new material and refine, refine, refine his act.

Here's some of the bad news: Colvin believes in something called the "10-year rule". What this means is that he believes that it can take 10-years to achieve a high level of excellence in just about any field. However, you can still do it. What it will take is deliberate practice. Two key activities are called for here: over practicing and getting feedback from others. One final point: Colvin says that if your job feels easy, then you are unlikely to ever become a star. Words to think about...

Chapter 2

How To Protect Your IT Career
From Sabotage

Chapter 2: How To Protect Your IT Career From Sabotage

They really are out to get you, you know. All those schemers who want your job, your promotion, your bonus are even as you read this sitting at their desk scheming how best to make you look bad, take credit for your work, or even how to get you fired. In this down economy, those who have it in for you are even more likely to take action because so many firms are in the process of trimming headcount that they want to save their jobs by taking yours. What's an IT leader to do?

Your career sabotage problems begin when you detect that someone is out to get you. Once you are aware that something is going on, it's going to bug the heck out of you. You are now officially in a bind: if you complain, then there is a good chance that you are going to be viewed as "... not being a team player", if you ignore it and do nothing, then you can pretty much kiss any future promotions goodbye.

So just what kind of actions do backstabbers take to bring you down? Here's a quick list – let's see how many of them you recognize as having been done to you either now or in the past:

Taking Credit For Your Work: this is a classic. The backstabber talks with you to find all about work that you have been doing and then represents that work to others as having been done by them. Sometimes they will even tell you that you've done a poor job and ask you to not talk about it so that you don't look foolish – and so they can take credit for it.

Spreading Rumors About You: this can be a sneaky one because it can go on for a long time without you knowing about it. If you have a good network, somebody besides you will probably hear about the rumors before you do and tell you. Otherwise you're just going to have to keep your ears open and detect what people seem to be saying about you.

Project Sabotage: In this case, the saboteur realizes that your career advancement depends on the project that you are in charge of being a success. Once they know this, they will be willing to work very hard to cause your project to fail. Withholding needed resources or providing needed information late are two easy ways to drill holes in your project boat.

It sure seems like it will be easy for others to sneak in to our rooms in the middle of the night and make off with our careers. Is there anything that we can do? It turns out that yes, there are things that you can do to protect yourself and your career. They aren't easy and they don't always work, but they sure are better than sitting around and waiting for the axe to fall on you because of the actions of others. Here are some thoughts:

Keep your cool: the last thing that you want to do is to flip out. If you let your temper get the better of you, then you'll have fewer options for solving the sabotage problem.

No Direct Confrontation: Look, if they've been clever enough to try to get you out of their way, then they've probably not left any evidence lying around. Even if you could get all CSI on them, you are in a workplace and nobody really cares about that piece of hair that you found that clearly shows that your saboteur was the one that spread the rumor that you were hard to get along with.

Make Sure The Rumors Are Not Correct: So this is just a bit awkward, is there a possibility that the rumors could be right? Take a moment to look in the mirror and do some hard thinking. If the stories are correct, then you've got other problems to solve.

Love Those Timestamps: people can only take credit for your work if nobody else knows that you did the work first (first come, first served). What this means is that email can be your new best friend. When you are reporting on results or completed work, send out an email telling as many people as possible. This way the world will know that you did the work and when you did it. This can stop a saboteur in his / her tracks.

Talk To Your Boss: At the end of the day, your boss is the one who really has control over your career. You need to have a talk with him/her and let them know what's going on and ask for their help in resolving it. After all, this is just the kind of personnel thing that bosses are there to take care of.

Talk To Your Boss' Boss: Of course, if it's your boss that is doing the backstabbing, you really need to get some outside help. Talking with his/her boss is one way to do this. Another way is to talk with someone else at that same level and ask them to intervene.

Of course, if it turns out that it's your boss that is doing your career in, you've got a real problem. There is a very good chance that in the end it's going to be either you or him/her once you start to put a stop to the sabotage. Make sure that your resume is up-to-date because there is a good chance that you just might be needing it soon…

Chapter 3

What Can Top Athletes Teach You About Being A Better IT Leader?

Chapter 3: What Can Top Athletes Teach You About Being A Better IT Leader?

So we all know that Tiger Woods is a fantastic golfer. However, do you think that he'd be any good at running an IT team? The answer, somewhat surprisingly, is that yes, he probably would do a good job. The reason is that there is a lot of similarity between being an excellent athlete and being a top-notch IT manager.

Graham Jones is the founder of a company called Lane4 which uses studies of professional athletes to help managers do a better job of managing. One of the interesting things that he has discovered is that in the area of sports, just like in the world of business, one of the main obstacles to achieving something that has been identified as being "impossible" just might be a self-limiting way of thinking.

One of the first things that you have to realize about being an IT leader is that great leaders are not born, but are rather made. Sure some leaders have nature gifts such as communication skills and leadership attributes; however, the most important skill that they need to have is mental toughness – this means that they get better at doing their job when things get tough.

Great IT leaders rise up not due to chance or luck, but rather because they planned to succeed. Specifically, they identified and achieved lots and lots of little goals in order to get to where they are. This requires them to sharpen their skills and to, much like Madonna, reinvent themselves many times in order to stay out in front of their peers.

So what can IT leaders learn from top athletes? Simple, how to succeed over and over again. Here are the steps that are needed to achieve top performance over and over again:

Gotta Learn To Love That Pressure

Call it what you like, but pressure is what drives great athletes and great IT leaders to achieve their best. What this means for you is that you've got to find a way to learn to love pressure. Another way to say this is that you've got to commit yourself to using work pressure to continually improve yourself all the time.

One secret to dealing effectively with pressure is to only focus on making yourself better. Don't let yourself get distracted by other IT leaders who manage / complete successful projects, get promoted, win awards, etc. Instead, focus on those things that you can control and don't spend any time thinking about the rest.

You need to be able to step away from the workplace pressure. This means that you actually do need to have another life – family / hobbies / sports, whatever. Top athletes have the ability to flip the pressure switch on when they are "on the job" and then flip it off when they are involved in their other life.

It's All About The Long Term

By the way, you will occasionally fail. This means that you need to have a way to pick yourself up, dust yourself off, and get back to work. A good way to be able to do this is to have long term goals that you focus on.

What star athletes do is to create very detailed plans that are made up of a series of short term goals. The plan is laid out so that the athlete can do his / her best at the right time – not peaking too early or too late. IT leaders need to do the same. You want to make sure that when you have a big success, it is the right time for it to get maximum exposure within the company.

Push Baby, Push!

We all push ourselves based on the people who we work directly with. If we are working with a bunch of slackers, then there won't be much self-pushing going on. Instead, we should be searching for opportunities to work with the best-of-the-best. This is very similar to when top athletes train with their fiercest competitors in order to push themselves to be their very best.

Invent And Then Reinvent Yourself

Always be sure to get feedback from trusted sources. This will allow you to understand what you are doing well and where you need to make changes. These changes will allow you to reinvent yourself so that you can become the best IT leader that you can be.

Party Like A Rock Star

Something that IT leaders all too often pass over is to take a break after a major achievement and celebrate. Spending as much effort celebrating a success as you did achieving the success is a way to reward yourself. This is the time to blow off some steam, pause and catch your breath before you push on to the next higher level.

Chapter 4

Should An IT Manger Be A "Secret Shopper" When Looking For A New Job?

Chapter 4: Should An IT Manger Be A "Secret Shopper" When Looking For A New Job?

So let's pretend for a moment that you are NOT fabulously satisfied with your current job as an IT Leader. You've decided that global recession or not, you really, really need to find yourself a new IT job. How do you plan on going about doing this? There is nothing new that I can tell you about Monster.com or Dice.com, writing the perfect resume, or even how to leverage social networks like LinkedIn in order to get an offer. Instead, let's talk about what you need to do AFTER you get the offer.

When you were just out of school, or when a job that you had suddenly went away, you probably went searching for the first job that would start providing you with a paycheck. However, times have changed. You now actually have a bit of a career going and, assuming that you currently have a job, you'd prefer to not muck it up.

What this means is that your search for you next IT Leader job needs to include a few additional steps that just might strike you as strange – but could very well save your career. Interested? Let's see what you need to do next.

Once you have an offer from a company, STOP! Don't accept it right off the bat. Tell the company that you need some time to consider their offer. Two days would be perfect, but you can even accomplish what you need to get done in a single day if you move quickly.

We all know that job descriptions are generally junk – originally created too long ago by someone who thought that they knew what they needed and then transformed into junk by caring members of the HR and legal teams so that nobody would be offended or even know what the job was about. This means that you need to make sure that you can get along with your potential new boss (hopefully you have already talked with him/her). Now you've got to find out if this COMPANY is the right company for you.

In a nutshell, if the company makes a lousy product / service and all of their customers are ticked off at them, then this is probably not the best place for you to take your career to. This is the new angle that you need to add to your job search: not just checking out the new job, but also checking out the company that you are considering joining.

How do you do this for an IT job? If the company that you are thinking about joining has retail stores or distributors that carry their products, then this part is easy – it's time to go shopping. If you were considering joining Bose's IT department, then you'd want to visit your local Best Buy and check out their home theater section.

Even more important than confirming that Bose products are still available (proof that they aren't going out of business), would be what you learned by talking to the sales associates. What do they think about Bose products? Do people return them? Are they selling well? Although these are not IT questions, they are critical to making sure that you are joining a growing, thriving company instead of a stalling, shrinking one.

If the company that you are thinking about joining does not have their products in retail stores, then you're going to have to be a bit more creative. Almost all firms have some sort of help / support line. Play the role of a customer and give it a call – how do they treat you? Do some on-line searching for reviews of the company and their products. Look for legal actions against the company – discrimination lawsuits are never a good thing.

At this stage in your IT career, you need to adopt a bigger view of the world when you go looking for your next job. It's no longer just about the job, but now it's also about the company that you might be working for...

Chapter 5

---

3 Secrets That Every IT Leader Needs To Know

Chapter 5: 3 Secrets That Every IT Leader Needs To Know

How does one become a good IT Leader? I mean really, are there college classes on this stuff? Do firms pick out a mentor for you once you get promoted to a management position? Or upon receiving a promotion to management are you allowed to view the magical book of management in which all secrets of team motivation and employee counseling are revealed? Nope.

I don't know how things are done where you work, but all too often hard working "individual contributors" are promoted into management positions pretty much overnight. They go from having a very clear idea of what they are supposed to be doing to having absolutely no clue as to what is going on.

Some people thrive in this type of situation. I like to think of them as being the IT field's equivalent of Weebles – they always seem to land standing up. However, for the rest of us, things are never so easy.

Wouldn't it be nice if there was some way for IT professionals to get management experience BEFORE they had to use it? Some sort of "lab" environment in which you could be a manager and try out different ways to manage a team in order to find out what works for you and what doesn't?

I've got some good news for you – there is such a "management lab" and it's basically free for the taking. I've got to be careful how I say this next part because I might lose you if you are reading this quickly – it's not what you think it is. The answer to your quest to try out and improve you management skills is: join Toastmasters.

HOLD ON! Don't stop reading – this is, somewhat surprisingly, not really about learning to speak in public. I'm not sure if you know what Toastmasters is, so I should explain. If you know what it is, then stay with me – there is more going on here than you may be aware of.

Toastmasters is an international organization that helps people become more competent and comfortable speaking in front of an audience. The nonprofit organization now has nearly 235,000 members in 11,700 clubs in 92 countries. Undoubtedly there is a club near where you are.

Yeah, yeah – Toastmasters is all about teaching its members how to speak effectively before groups of people. This is actually an important skill for all IT leaders to have. If you can't address your team / department, then you are going to be at a severe disadvantage when it comes to motivating and directing your teams. However, there is a lot more to why you should join Toastmasters...

Toastmasters is organized into "clubs" that are sprinkled just about everywhere. Each club has a group of about seven elected offices who run and organize the club. From the president down to the treasure these folks are effectively running a small business. Club member dues are collected and then the money is used to run the club for the next 6 months.

Club officers have to deal with staffing issues, securing locations for meetings, retaining club members, motivating members to reach goals, and basically keeping everyone in line. Oh, there is one additional point – nobody "works" for Toastmasters at the club level. Instead, everyone is a volunteer. This means that management by force ("do it or I'll fire you") won't work. Toastmaster officers need to find ways to motivate people to do things for them.

On a third level, each Toastmasters meeting is run by a rotating club member. This person is responsible for the entire meeting – picking a location, scheduling speakers, and filling meeting specific duty roles, and making sure that everything stays on time. This is just like a standard business meeting except that nobody works for anyone else so once again motivation is the key to success.

In the end, Toastmasters operates on three different levels: teaching public speaking skills, club management training, and how to run successful meetings. All of this is available to you for about $30 every 6 months.

So what happens if you join, get a leadership position, and then proceed to screw it up? Nothing. What will probably happen is that other club members who have had the position that you are in will step in and (1) tell you what you've done wrong, and (2) help you to correct it. That's it – nobody gets "fired".

Now if you screw up your new IT management position, I can't say that you won't get fired. Perhaps it's time to check out Toastmasters and see if it can help you to become the successful IT leader that we all know that you can be…?

Chapter 6

What's An IT Manger To Do When You Screw-Up BIG TIME?

Chapter 6: What's An IT Manger To Do When You Screw-Up BIG TIME?

So I'll be the first one to admit it – I've screwed up big time at work. It was awhile back, but as I remember it I was responsible for crunching some numbers that were going into a report that was being used to plan what the company was going to be working on for the next year. Somehow I forgot to include some critical numbers. I discovered my mistake. What should I have done next?

As IT Leaders, we'd like to appear as though we never make mistakes to both our superiors as well as to our teams. However, the sad reality is that we do screw-up and sometimes in a big way. What hurts the most about doing things like this is that it flies in the face of how we view ourselves (as perfect). The fancy name for what this creates is called "cognitive dissonance".

Phyllis Korkki has looked into this situation in a piece that she wrote for the New York Times and to get to the heart of the matter she talked with the social psychologist Carol Travis (author of Mistakes Were Made (But Not by Me): Why We Justify Foolish Beliefs, Bad Decisions, and Hurtful Acts). What Travis says is that internally we look at what we've done and we say to ourselves "There is no way that I could have screwed-up on something that I view myself as being good at." Once we have this thought, then our mind moves on and starts to come up with various forms of self-justification for what we've gone and done. How do we do this? You pick: lies, blame, defensiveness, etc.

So this might be a bad situation to find yourself in, but what can you possibly do to make it worse? Simple – don't tell anyone and try to cover it up. Just in case you haven't learned your lesson from Enron, Worldcom, or most recently Satyam over in

India then listen and understand. Covering up your error will lead to bigger and bigger problems that will eventually entangle you so securely that you can't get free. Talk about stress!

So once you've made the mistake, what SHOULD you do? First off, realize that this mistake is not necessarily a reflection of either your intelligence or your talents. If you can realize this, then you should be able to mentally separate who you are as a person from this event.

What next? Ok – so this is the tough part. You need to point out your error sooner than later. The first step in doing this is to go to the people whom your error has affected and do that most painful of all actions, apologize.

Your next step has to be to get to work undoing the damage that you've done and fixing the situation that you've caused. This is not easy to do either, but you should realize that it's the right thing to do. It turns out that keeping the knowledge that you've screwed something up inside will be a bigger burden than just getting it out into the open.

What if I get fired? Well that's always a possibility; however, wouldn't you rather go out because you pointed out something that you did instead of being found out by someone else? It's all a matter of who you want to be in control of your life.

A lot rests on how your boss deals with your slip up. If he / she is going to get ticked off, then you are going to be a lot less likely to point it out. As an IT Leader you need to realize that how your team views you will also determine if they feel comfortable coming to you when they screw up (and they will).

Hopefully your boss will realize that having you point out your mistake earlier rather than later is a good thing. Hey, if you've got a worker who is pointing out their mistakes to you then that's a very good thing. If it keeps happening over and over again, then you need to move the person to a different position.

In my case, my boss turned out to be incredibly cool. He sighed because he realized that his management was not going to be happy about the correction that was going to be required and then he went and "fell on the sword" – he accepted blame for my mistake. Talk about building loyalty! Man, I double and triple checked everything that I gave him after that and I would have gladly fallen on the sword for him...

Chapter 7

IT Leader Job Hunting Secrets

Chapter 7: IT Leader Job Hunting Secrets

So I like to talk about how to be a better IT Leader just as much as the next guy, but what are you supposed to do **when your job has gone away?** I've been getting a lot of email from IT managers who are finding themselves unintentionally "in-between jobs" for the first time in a long time. The first thing to realize is that no matter how long it takes to find the next job this is just temporary. The next thing to understand is that there are secrets to speeding up the finding of your next IT job...

The #1 problem that I see in IT managers that I'm working with who are searching for a new job after having lost their last one is that for the first time in a long time **they don't know what to do with their time**. When they were working it seemed like they never had enough of the stuff. However, now that their job has gone away, they don't know what to do with themselves.

The first thing that we all need to realize is that you're going to need is some **structure in your life** if you want to hurry up the process of finding your next job. If you don't have any structure to how you are spending your day, then you won't be organized and you won't be focused. This means that you won't be able to get to where you want to go.

Job Hunting Is Like Having Another Job

When I've been between IT jobs, it took way too long for me to have this mental breakthrough: **job hunting IS my job**. When you have this understanding, a lot of other things start to fall into place. Just like any IT job that you've had in past, you need to structure your new job hunting job so that you have specific work hours and a schedule for getting things done along with deadlines.

The secret to making your job hunt a success is to treat it like **a full-time job**. This means that you're going to have to do things like set aside some physical space for your job hunting work: that's exactly what your home office was created for.

All too often immediately after having lost an IT job, we'll sit down, sign onto Monster.com, and **start applying for every job that we can find**. Don't do this.

Instead, go about starting your job search in the right way. The first thing that you are going to want to do is take some time to get **well organized**. This means that you're going have to start off by taking the time to spend several days or even as long as a week to really get set up for your job search.

Getting set up means doing several things that are important to do, but **not necessarily related to applying for any one specific job opening**. Instead, you need to spend your time getting your resume in order, maybe creating some cover letter templates, even chasing down some good references would be time well spent.

The Three Bucket System

Face it, when you suddenly find yourself running a one person business in which you have to do everything, it's pretty easy to reach a point where you just throw your hands up in the air and say "I give up!" Don't do it. Julie Morgenstern a productivity author suggests that you view your day as being divided up into **three separate compartments**: preparation and research, meetings, and follow-up.

Her main point is that it is dangerous for us to spend too much time doing **any one thing**. What we need to do is to try to schedule a meeting every day (or at least five meetings a week).

Instead of spending all of your time hunched over your laptop, this will help to keep you better connected to the outside world.

Julie also suggests that we end every day by **planning the next one, plus the two days after that**. This sets up a time horizon where we start to feel as though we know what's coming up and so it's not so scary. Face it, we are energized by getting things done and this will help us do that.

What All Of This Means For You

Losing an IT job is **never good**, losing an IT manager's job is even worse. It's all too easy to get lost in feeling bad for ourselves when this occurs.

The experts tell us that we need to sit ourselves down and realize that **we have a new job**: finding our next job. Getting organized and coming up with ways to divide up our days into productive segments will help us to get there.

The most important thing to remember when you are hunting for your next job is that **you will find it**. The only thing that you can't control is how long it will take. Use these suggestions that we've discussed and that hunt will take less time!

Chapter 8

Shh! How To Keep Your IT Job Search Secret...

Chapter 8: Shh! How To Keep Your IT Job Search Secret...

Do you plan on working at your current IT job forever? Nope, I didn't think so. In fact, there's a very good chance that you won't be working for the company that you are currently working at forever. What this means is that you've got to start that search for your next job now. Oh, and you've got to keep it a secret...

Sometimes we IT leaders get just a little bit too caught up in ourselves. This happens when we think that our technical skills or job experience will do the speaking for us when we next go looking for a job. Bad news, finding your next job won't happen this way.

The key to a successful IT Leader's job search is to prepare for your next job long before it becomes necessary to go looking for it. You know what I'm going to say next: you've got to keep up with what's going on in your professional network. This network needs to include people both inside your current company as well as outside it. Keeping up with your network is important because you don't want your networking activities to suddenly trigger suspicion among your coworkers.

It is possible to keep the search for your next job invisible. The key is to make sure that you are always meeting with professional contacts, attending industry gatherings, and (of course) being active on social networking sites.

This being said, you can overdo the social networking thing. For example, in LinkedIn, updates or changes to your account are sent out to your contacts. Fellow workers may start to notice it if you all of a sudden you start to gather new recommendations to your LinkedIn account. Not just social networking can be a tip off, if you dramatically improve how you dress in order to combine your current job with interviews, then your coworkers are certain to notice.

This all leads to the most delicate of questions: when should you tell your current boss that you are planning on leaving? I can answer this one for you: as late in the process as possible. Since you can never really be sure how your current employer is going to react to your announcement that you are leaving, it's best to provide yourself with as much time to get your act together as possible. My suggestion here is to make it so that if after you make your announcement your boss blows his / her top and angrily orders you to leave the building, you are ready for it.

The second most delicate question has to do with what you should say if your company (or boss) conducts an exit interview with you. When I left my first job, I was young and naive. When they asked me what I would have changed in my old department, I opened up with both barrels. Not a good idea!

Only as I've grown older have I come to realize that the real purpose of an exit interview is to detect if the company is going to be facing any discrimination lawsuits. What you say about your boss / department / job might get written down, but in the end it probably won't have much of an impact.

So there you go, IT Leaders should always be searching for their next job. This search should involve talking with real people as well as connecting online. You can keep this search a secret for as long as you want it to be, but make sure that you prepare to leave before you tell your boss that you are leaving!

Chapter 9

So IT Leader, Are You Thinking About Getting An Executive MBA...?

Chapter 9: So IT Leader, Are You Thinking About Getting An Executive MBA...?

As the world's economy continues to shudder, everyone in IT is scrambling to find ways to make themselves more valuable to both their current employer as well as to their next employer (if needed). For a long time, getting an MBA has been an option that many IT Leaders have considered. The big drawback has always been the amount of time that this degree requires – on top of all of your other responsibilities. It turns out that there is another option: the executive MBA.

I guess a good question to start off with is how does an executive MBA differ from a "regular" MBA? An executive MBA generally meets every other weekend for two full days – Friday and Saturday. Students generally travel to campus to participate in classes. While not in class, remotely located students collaborate to complete class assignments.

There's also the issue of time: an executive MBA generally takes two years from start to finish. If you are working and choose to participate in a regular MBA, there's a good chance that it will end up taking you longer to complete your degree as you take one or two classes a semester.

Where to go is the big question if you choose to pursue an executive MBA. There are a lot of executive MBA programs out there and because they are such a profit center for universities, they are all marketed heavily. Thankfully the folks over at the Wall Street Journal have taken the time to conduct a survey and they've found the best places for an IT Leader to go.

Just how do you go about ranking executive MBA programs? Well over at the WSJ they decided to go about doing it based on multiple criteria. The most important factor that they chose was how corporations viewed the programs – I mean you're really getting the degree to boost your marketability, right? Next came how students in the program actually felt about the program. Finally, the value of what they were being taught was factored in.

So who won? Here's the ranking of the top 10 executive MBA programs as computed by the Wall Street Journal:

1. Northwestern University (Kellogg)
2. University of Pennsylvania (Wharton)
3. Thunderbird School of Global Management
4. University of Southern California (Marshall)
5. University of North Carolina (Kenan-Flagler)
6. University of Michigan (Ross)
7. Cornell University (Johnson)
8. Columbia University (NY Program)
9. University of Chicago
10. Duke University (Fuqua)

So what do YOU need to consider if you are thinking about enrolling in an executive MBA program above and beyond which program ranks the highest? One interesting point is just how much this is going to cost.

The executive MBA programs that were reviewed by the Wall Street Journal cost between $65,000 and $160,000 just in tuition (books, travel, etc. would all be extra). Since lots of students work for firms that pay all/part of the cost of the program, the median out-of-pocket cost turned out to be something like $45,000. Of course then there's the issue of travel...

In the survey, 64% of the executive MBA students traveled less than 50 miles to go to school which means most of them are local to the school. However 7% traveled up to 200 miles and 9% traveled more than 1,000 miles.

In the end, the big question is if this is all worth it? Once again we can go back to the survey to find out. 24% of those students surveyed said that they had been given a both a raise and a promotion since they started executive MBA classes. Another 30% said that they expect both in the next year.

Chapter 10

How IT Managers Can Get Better At Creating Powerpoint Slides

Chapter 10: How IT Managers Can Get Better At Creating Powerpoint Slides

Yeah, yeah I know that everyone says that they hate PowerPoint – "death by PowerPoint" and all of that. However, the reality of a modern IT Manger's life is that we end up using PowerPoint to communicate a lot of information about our departments and the current status of our projects. Until you rise high enough in the organization to have someone on staff who creates your presentations for you, you're going to be stuck doing this yourself. Thank goodness you took all of those PowerPoint classes back in college…

What? You've never had a PowerPoint class in your life? Hmm, can I at least assume that you know about the color wheel? Dang – struck out there also? Looks like we're going to have to have a talk here.

There are some people out there that are really gifted artists. One that comes to mind is the Duarte design team over at slide:ology. However, then there is the rest of us. PowerPoint has a bunch of flashy features that lots of people like to use; however, the key is to remember that it's really a communication tool. This means that you'd like to get good enough at using it that you can get your point across in a clear way that will stick with your audience.

So how does an IT manager go about doing this? It's actually pretty simple – it will just take an investment in time. I would suggest that you find a PowerPoint presentation that you've seen that really worked for you – it communicated what it was trying to say in a concise, clear way. Then you need to sit down with a blank PowerPoint presentation and try to recreate it from scratch.

This is actually a lot harder than it might seem at first, getting all of the details of a presentation that someone else created (fonts, colors, line thicknesses, what goes on top of what else, etc.) can be a challenge. However, as you go through this copy / creation process you'll discover how a really good presentation comes together.

Chapter 11

IT Managers & The Secret Of The Color Wheel

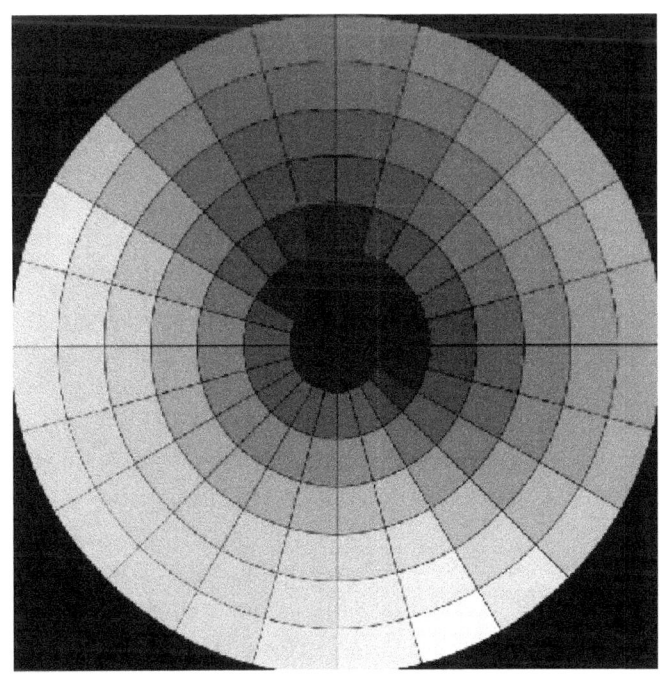

Chapter 11: IT Managers & The Secret Of The Color Wheel

So I'm just a little bit off the beaten path with this discussion, but I've recently had to sit through so many bad presentations that I'm feeling an overwhelming need to try to make the world a better place for PowerPoint slides to live in.

We all live and die by PowerPoint. I can't begin to tell you how many bosses that I've had that insisted that I provide them with status updates in PowerPoint form. What part of my hero Edward Tuff's write up after the Space Shuttle Challenger disaster ("PowerPoint") did they not read?

Well no matter, we have to do what we have to do. However, at the very least we should be able to do it to the best of our ability. One of the greatest errors that I've been seeing as of late is the criminal use of colors that in no way should ever be used together. Look, I realize that for most of us (guys) getting dressed in the morning can be a challenge (what goes with what), but we should have the same level of concern when it comes to creating slides.

So how should an IT manger pick colors for his/her PowerPoint slides? Simple – use a color wheel. Using a color wheel and just a bit of color theory, a product manager can start to produce professional looking slides. It turns out that using analogous colors (colors that are next to each other on the color wheel) or complementary colors (colors are across from each other on the color wheel) are easy ways to get your colors right.

Thanks to the Internet, there are now free sites that if you need to start with one color (company color, department color) will allow you to find out what colors work with that color. If this all seems to be too much for you, then you can visit the Colors On

The Web site and press the button in order to get a random color scheme that has matching colors created for you.

Chapter 12

How Should IT Leaders Use Outplacement Services?

Chapter 12: How Should IT Leaders Use Outplacement Services?

Dang it, you've been let go. It really doesn't matter the reason why – just the fact that your (former) employer decided that they **could get along without** your services can really sting. However, before the door swings close behind you for the last time, the ball is in still in your court and you need to know what to do with it.

As IT Leaders, we are a pretty arrogant bunch. A recent survey by the global outsourcing firm Right Management found that seven out of 10 job seekers thought that **they knew exactly what they needed to do** in order to land their next job. However, once they went through the outplacement service, that number dropped down to two.

At most firms, when a layoff sweeps through and you get caught up in it, you will be offered the services of an **outplacement firm**. Many of us poo-poo this because for one reason or another we think that it won't be of any help to us. That's where you'd be wrong.

If you find yourself in this position, here's what you need to do in order to make the most of the outplacement service that has been offered to you:

Don't Drag Your Feet: You've been let go, get over it and don't delay starting to use your outplacement service. The longer you wait, the more competition you will face.

Pick Your Consultant Carefully: You can always ask to meet with a different consultant so make sure that the one that you've got is the right one for you. Consider things like track record, background, experience in your industry, and of course their current workload.

Do Your Homework: You'll probably be asked to complete personality tests and career assignments. Do them! This is the time for you to make sure that the next job that you get is really the right one for you.

Stuff Yourself: The outplacement firm probably offers many different types of classes, workshops, seminars, and networking events. This is your best chance to find out if things have changed and if your type of job is now located in different parts of other firms.

Don't Work Remotely: Although in this day and age it is possible to work with your counselor online, try not to. Instead go into the office and meet with them face-to-face. This will help to build a stronger relationship with them and who knows what other professionals you'll meet there.

Nothing can make the initial pain of being let go from your IT job hurt less. However, as with so many things in life, the pain fades over time. You need to make sure that you get moving right off the bat so that by the time your pain has faded, **you are already in your next job**.

Hard work does not
guarantee success;
However, success does
not happen
without hard work.

- Dr. Jim Anderson

Create IT Departments That Are Productive And A Valuable Asset To The Rest Of The Company!

Dr. Jim Anderson is available to provide training and coaching on the topics that are the most important to people who have to manage IT departments: how can I build a productive IT department (and keep it together) while at the same time providing the rest of the company with the IT services that they need?

Dr. Anderson believes that in order to both learn and remember what he says, speakers need to laugh. Each one of his speeches is full of fun and humor so that what he says "sticks" with everyone.

Dr. Anderson's CIO Skills Training Includes:

1. How to identify and attract the right type of IT workers to your IT department.
2. How to build relationships with the company's senior management in order to get the support that you need?
3. How to stay on top of changing technology and security issues so that you never get surprised?

Dr. Jim Anderson works with over 100 customers per year. To invite Dr. Anderson to work with you, contact him at:

Phone: 813-418-6970 or
Email: jim@BlueElephantConsulting.com

Blue Elephant Consulting

Speaking   Negotiating   Managing   Marketi

Photo Credits:

Cover - Donnie Ray Jones

https://www.flickr.com/photos/donnieray/

Chapter 1 - Keith Allison

https://www.flickr.com/photos/keithallison/

Chapter 2 - Dieter Drescher

https://www.flickr.com/photos/cosmosfan/

Chapter 3 – Sangudo

https://www.flickr.com/photos/sangudo/

Chapter 4 - Fred Seibert

https://www.flickr.com/photos/84568447@N00/

Chapter 5 - Amy Stephenson

https://www.flickr.com/photos/24013072@N05/

Chapter 6 - My Sideways World

https://www.flickr.com/photos/40529684@N00/

Chapter 7 - m01229

https://www.flickr.com/photos/39908901@N06/

Chapter 8 - kate Hiscock

https://www.flickr.com/photos/slightlyeverything/

Chapter 9 - Me-Liss-A

https://www.flickr.com/photos/lissjasmin/

Chapter 10 - AJC1

https://www.flickr.com/photos/ajc1/

Chapter 11 - Robson#

https://www.flickr.com/photos/_robson_/

Chapter 12 - Krishna De

https://www.flickr.com/photos/krishnade/

Other Books By The Author

Product Management

- How Product Managers Can Sell More Of Their Product: Tips & Techniques For Product Managers To Better Understand How To Sell Their Product

- How Product Managers Can Sell More Of Their Product: Tips & Techniques For Product Managers To Better Understand How To Sell Their Product

- How To Create A Successful Product That Customers Will Want: Techniques For Product Managers To Boost Product Sales And Increase Customer Satisfaction

- What Product Managers Need To Know About World-Class Product Development: How Product Managers Can Create Successful Products

- How Product Managers Can Learn To Understand Their Customers: Techniques For Product Managers To Better Understand What Their Customers Really Want

- Product Management Secrets: Techniques For Product Managers To Boost Product Sales And Increase Customer Satisfaction

- Product Development Lessons For Product Managers: How Product Managers Can Create Successful Products

- Customer Lessons For Product Managers: Techniques For Product Managers To Better Understand What Their Customers Really Want

- Product Failure Lessons For Product Managers: Examples Of Products That Have Failed For Product Managers To Learn From

- Communication Skills For Product Managers: The Communication Skills That Product Managers Need To Know How To Use In Order To Have A Successful Product

- How To Have A Successful Product Manager Career: The Things That You Need To Be Doing TODAY In Order To Have A Successful Product Manager Career

- Product Manager Product Success: How to keep your product on track and make it become a success

Public Speaking

- Creating Speeches That Work: How To Create A Speech That Will Make Your Message Be Remembered Forever!

- How To Organize A Speech In Order To Make Your Point: How to put together a speech that will capture and hold your audience's attention

- Changing How You Speak To Overcome Your Fear Of Speaking: Change techniques that will transform a speech into a memorable event

- Delivering Excellence: How To Give Presentations That Make A Difference: Presentation techniques that will transform a speech into a memorable event

- Tools Speakers Need In Order To Give The Perfect Speech: What tools to use to create your next speech so that your message will be remembered forever!

- How To Create A Speech That Will Be Remembered

- Secrets To Organizing A Speech For Maximum Impact: How to put together a speech that will capture and hold your audience's attention

- How To Become A Better Speaker By Changing How You Speak: Change techniques that will transform a speech into a memorable event

- How To Give A Great Presentation: Presentation techniques that will transform a speech into a memorable event

- How To Rehearse In Order To Give The Perfect Speech: How to effectively rehearse your next speech to that your message be remembered forever!

- Secrets To Creating The Perfect Speech: How to create a speech that will make your message be remembered forever!

- Secrets To Organizing The Perfect Speech: How to organize the best speech of your life!

- Secrets To Planning The Perfect Speech: How to plan to give the best speech of your life

- How To Show What You Mean During A Presentation: How to use visual techniques to transform a speech into a memorable event

CIO Skills

- How CIOs Can Bring Business And IT Together: How CIOs Can Use Their Technical Skills To Help Their Company Solve Real-World Business Problems

- New IT Technology Issues Facing CIOs: How CIOs Can Stay On Top Of The Changes In The Technology That Powers The Company

- Keeping The Barbarians Out: How CIOs Can Secure Their Department and Company: Tips And Techniques For CIOs To Use In Order To Secure Both Their IT Department And Their Company

- What CIOs Need To Know In Order To Successfully Manage An IT Department: Decision Making Skills That Every CIO Needs To Have In Order To Be Able To Make The Right Choices

- Becoming A Powerful And Effective Leader: Tips And Techniques That IT Managers Can Use In Order To Develop Leadership Skills

- CIO Secrets For Growing Innovation: Tips And Techniques For CIOs To Use In Order To Make Innovation Happen In Their IT Department

- Your Success As A CIO Depends On How Well You Communicate: Tips And Techniques For CIOs To

Use In Order To Become Better Communicators

- What CIOs Need To Know About Working With Partners: Techniques For CIOs To Use In Order To Be Able To Successfully Work With Partners

- Critical CIO Management Skills: Decision Making Skills That Every CIO Needs To Have In Order To Be Able To Make The Right Choices

- How CIOs Can Make Innovation Happen: Tips And Techniques For CIOs To Use In Order To Make Innovation Happen In Their IT Department

- CIO Communication Skills Secrets: Tips And Techniques For CIOs To Use In Order To Become Better Communicators

- Managing Your CIO Career: Steps That CIOs Have To Take In Order To Have A Long And Successful Career

- CIO Business Skills: How CIOs can work effectively with the rest of the company!

IT Manager Skills

- How IT Managers Can Use New Technology To Meet Today's IT Challenges: Technologies That IT

Managers Can Use In Order to Make Their Teams More Productive

- How To Build High Performance IT Teams: Tips And Techniques That IT Managers Can Use In Order To Develop Productive Teams

- Save Yourself, Save Your Job – How To Manage Your IT Career: Secrets That IT Managers Can Use In Order To Have A Successful Career

- Growing Your CIO Career: How CIOs Can Work With The Entire Company In Order To Be Successful

- How IT Managers Can Make Innovation Happen: Tips And Techniques For IT Managers To Use In Order To Make Innovation Happen In Their Teams

- Staffing Skills IT Managers Must Have: Tips And Techniques That IT Managers Can Use In Order To Correctly Staff Their Teams

- Secrets Of Effective Leadership For IT Managers: Tips And Techniques That IT Managers Can Use In Order To Develop Leadership Skills

- IT Manager Career Secrets: Tips And Techniques That IT Managers Can Use In Order To Have A

Successful Career

- IT Manager Budgeting Skills: How IT Managers Can Request, Manage, Use, And Track Their Funding

- Secrets Of Managing Budgets: What IT Managers Need To Know In Order To Understand How Their Company Uses Money

Negotiating

- Getting What You Want In A Negotiation By Learning How To Signal: How To Develop The Skill Of Effective Signaling In A Negotiation In Order To Get The Best Possible Outcome

- Exploring How To Get The Deal That You Want In A Negotiation: How To Develop The Skill Of Exploring What Is Possible In A Negotiation In Order To Reach The Best Possible Deal

- Use The Power Of Arguing To Win Your Next Negotiation: How To Develop The Skill Of Effective Arguing In A Negotiation In Order To Get The Best Possible Outcome

- Learn How To Signal In Your Next Negotiation: How To Develop The Skill Of Effective Signaling In A Negotiation In Order To Get The Best Possible

Outcome

- Learn The Skill Of Exploring In A Negotiation: How To Develop The Skill Of Exploring What Is Possible In A Negotiation In Order To Reach The Best Possible Deal

- Learn How To Argue In Your Next Negotiation: How To Develop The Skill Of Effective Arguing In A Negotiation In Order To Get The Best Possible Outcome|

- How To Open Your Next Negotiation: How To Start A Negotiation In Order To Get The Best Possible Outcome

- Preparing For Your Next Negotiation: What You Need To Do BEFORE A Negotiation Starts In Order To Get The Best Possible Deal

- Learn How To Package Trades In Your Next Negotiation

- All Good Things Come To An End: How To Close A Negotiation - How To Develop The Skill Of Closing In Order To Get The Best Possible Outcome From A Negotiation

- Take No Prisoners In Your Next Negotiation: How To Start A Negotiation In Order To Get The Best Possible Outcome

Miscellaneous

- How To Heal A Broken Leg – Fast!: Understanding how to deal with a broken leg in order to start walking again quickly

- How Software Defined Networking (SDN) Is Going To Change Your World Forever: The Revolution In Network Design And How It Affects You

- The Power Of Virtualization: How It Affects Memory, Servers, and Storage: The Revolution In Creating Virtual Devices And How It Affects You

- The Internet-Enabled Successful School District Superintendent: How To Use The Internet To Boost Parental Involvement In Your Schools

- Power Distribution Unit (PDU) Secrets: What Everyone Who Works In A Data Center Needs To Know!

- Making The Jump: How To Land Your Dream Job When You Get Out Of College!

- How To Use The Internet To Create Successful Students And Involved Parents

"Tips And Techniques That IT Managers Can Use In Order To Have A Successful Career"

This book has been written with one goal in mind – to show you how an IT manager can successfully manage their career. It's not easy being an IT manager so we're going to show you what you need to be doing in order to determine where you want your career to go and how to get there!

Let's Make Your IT Career A Success!

What You'll Find Inside:

- **HOW TO PROTECT YOUR IT CAREER FROM SABOTAGE**

- **WHAT CAN TOP ATHLETES TEACH YOU ABOUT BEING A BETTER IT LEADER?**

- **SHH! HOW TO KEEP YOUR IT JOB SEARCH SECRET...**

- **IT MANAGERS & THE SECRET OF THE COLOR WHEEL**

Dr. Jim Anderson brings his 25 years of real-world experience to this book. He's been an IT manager at some of the world's largest firms. He's going to show you what you need to do (and not do!) in order to successfully manage your career!

www.ingramcontent.com/pod-product-compliance
Lightning Source LLC
Chambersburg PA
CBHW071803170526
45167CB00003B/1148